EDGE BOOKS

Not Your Ordinary Trivia

W9-BYL-608

VIDEO GAME TRIVIA

What You Never Knew About Popular Games, Design Secrets, and the Coolest Characters

by Sean McCollum

CAPSTONE PRESS
a capstone imprint

Edge Books are published by Capstone Press,
1710 Roe Crest Drive, North Mankato, Minnesota 56003
www.mycapstone.com

Library of Congress Cataloging-in-Publication Data
Names: McCollum, Sean author.
Title: Video game trivia : what you never knew about popular games, design
   secrets, and the coolest characters / by Sean McCollum.
Description: North Mankato, Minnesota : Edge Books are published by
Capstone
   Press, [2019] | Series: Edge Books. Not your ordinary trivia | Includes
   webography. | Includes bibliographical references and index.
Identifiers: LCCN 2018005781 (print) | LCCN 2018010125 (ebook) | ISBN
   9781543525359 (eBook PDF) | ISBN 9781543525397 (ePub Fixed Layout) |
   ISBN 9781543525274 (library binding : alk. paper) | ISBN 9781543525311
   (paperback : alk. paper)
Subjects: LCSH: Video games—Miscellanea—Juvenile literature.
Classification: LCC GV1469.3 (ebook) | LCC GV1469.3 .M3839 2019 (print) |
DDC
   794.8—dc23
LC record available at https://lccn.loc.gov/2018005781

Editorial Credits
Mandy Robbins, editor; Juliette Peters, designer; Jo Miller, media researcher;
Tori Abraham, production specialist

Photo Credits
Alamy: Archive PL, 8b, Game Shots, 17, Marc Tielemans, 16, Pete Jenkins, 19 (inset), razorpix, 18, 20t; AP Images : Paul Sakuma, 11t; Getty Images: Sascha Steinbach/Stringer, 7; Newscom: imageBROKER/Jochen Tack, 12, KRT/MBR, 21t, REUTERS/Issei Kato, 13b, REUTERS/Jason Redmond, 15; Shutterstock: Africa Studio, 11b, alphaspirit, 4-5, Anna Chernova, cover (clouds), bestv, 6r, Bobnevv, 27, chrnsitr, 10, chuckchee, cover (game scene), CREATISTA, 22, Dan Thornberg, 8t, Dikiiy, 29, evgeny kondrashov, 24b, furtseff, 26b, hedgehog111, 6l, Jeramey Lende, 9t, Matthew Corley, 28t, OlegDoroshin, 14t, OleksandrO, 23b, ostill, 13t, Pavel L Photo and Video, 25, Pe3k, 9b, Refluo, 14b, rkl_foto, 26t, Roman Kosolapov, 23t, Shaun Robinson, 19t, Tinseltown, 20b, Untashable, 32, vipman, 19b, winui, 28b, xiaorui, 21b; U.S. Marine Corps photo by Cpl. Demetrius Morgan, 24t

Design Elements
Shutterstock: Anna Chernova, chuckchee, Untashable

Printed in the United States of America.
PA017

TABLE OF CONTENTS

Video Game Revolution

What were the first words ever said in a video game?

What game lets you play as a giant hand?

How can playing video games give your doctor an edge?

Keep reading to learn the answers to these questions and more. Video games have come a long way in a short time. Just 50 years ago, today's technology was only a dream. Electronics and computer experts have turned it into reality.

Today's video games combine art, music, filmmaking, and storytelling. Powerful software programs let you enter worlds beyond the imagination. In addition to gaming, this tech is being used to train workers for the future.

There is no telling where the video game revolution will lead. But it's fun to know where it came from.

CHAPTER 1

GREAT MOMENTS IN GAMING TECH

Electronics whizzes started making simple video games in the 1950s. *Bertie the Brain* was one of the first. It could play tic-tac-toe.

What goes great with video games? Pizza! Nolan Bushnell saw the future and a fortune on a video game screen. He and partner Ted Dabney **founded** Atari. Atari was one of the first electronic game makers. But Bushnell didn't stop there. He later launched Chuck E. Cheese **arcades**. These electronic funhouses combine pizza and video games—a brilliant combination.

found—to set up or start something

arcade—a business with video games that you pay to use

0:2

Allan Alcorn designed Atari's first hit game. He programmed *Pong*. It was a simple electronic table tennis match that made a beeping noise. It was also the first popular video game to include sound effects.

In 1972–73, *Pong* was released in arcades. People loved it and its simple sound effects. A home version soon followed and sold like crazy.

"Strike! Ball! Out!" Those were the first words a video game ever uttered. They called the action in Intellivision's *Major League Baseball*. The game was released in 1979. High-tech **sound cards** didn't become part of game systems until 1989. Then video games really started making noise.

sound card—computer hardware that allows software programs to produce sounds

Early video game programmers weren't always men. Dona Bailey was one of the women pioneers in the video game revolution. She teamed with Ed Logg to create and design the 1981 arcade game, *Centipede.* It was a hit! She became a college instructor of game design, teaching future designers.

Today's game consoles have tons of computing power. NASA's first space shuttle launched in 1981. Its flight computer had less than 1 percent of the computing power of 2005's Xbox 360 game console. The power of the 2017 Xbox One X has 24 times the computing power of the Xbox 360. More computing power means better computer **graphics** and faster play.

> **graphic**—a visual image such as an illustration, photograph, or work of art

Old video game graphics seem blocky compared to current graphics. More powerful computers made better graphics possible. Designers use polygons to build characters and scenes. The more polygons they can use, the clearer the image is. The first *Crash Bandicoot* had about 512 polygons in 1996. Recent characters like Nathan Drake in *Uncharted 4: A Thief's End* (2016) have about 90,000 polygons.

CHAPTER 2

GAME CHANGERS

Video games have gone from simple fun to high-powered action and strategy. Check out some wild facts about classic games.

The Japanese game-making company Square was about to go out of business in 1987. They were sure their new game would be their last. That's why they called it *Final Fantasy*. They should have called it *First and Forever Fantasy*. More than 30 years later, the series is going strong. There are more than 15 *Final Fantasy* titles. The game has also inspired movies and TV shows.

Madden NFL is the best-selling sports video game ever. Nothing else comes close. It is named for John Madden, a Hall of Fame football

coach. The game updates player rosters every year. The game is so lifelike, NFL quarterbacks Drew Brees and Teddy Bridgewater play it. They use the video game to drill their team's playbook.

Video games can inspire new words, such as "exergaming."
Dance, Dance Revolution helped coin that term because of the
workout it gives players. Some schools even feature *DDR* in gym
classes. On "difficult mode," the game lets a player burn almost
25 calories per three-minute song.

Guitar Hero: Aerosmith was released in 2008. It sold more than 3 million copies by 2010. Sales of the rock band's music jumped 40 percent afterward. The game helped **reboot** Aerosmith's fame.

reboot—to start something again

Mortal Kombat could turn the most peace-loving player into a fighter. However, the battles could get a little too intense for young gamers. In 1991 that game and others caused lawmakers to create the Entertainment Software Rating Board, or ESRB. This system rates video games like movies. Ratings go from "E for Everyone" to "M for Mature Audiences."

In 2006 Wii popularized a gaming system that let players actually swing, throw, and punch using motion-sensing technology. The first five games featured on *Wii Sports* were tennis, baseball, bowling, boxing, and golf. Today, there are more than 1,200 titles playable on Wii. They range from *Alice in Wonderland* to *All-Star Karate*. Wii consoles rank among the best-sellers of all time.

Angry Birds features feathered friends battling green pigs. It has been the top-selling paid **app** at the online App Store for years. *Angry Birds Space* and *Angry Birds Seasons* have also been in the top 10. The game has spun off a movie and several TV series.

"Electronic sports," or eSports, is gaining a big following. It has more than 300 million fans worldwide who watch as well as play. For professional gamers, *Defense of the Ancients 2* (*Dota2*) has been the game of choice. *Dota2* champ Saahil "Universe" Arora of the United States earned his first $1 million by age 25.

In Japan, *Dragon Quest* remains a classic role-playing game. The first game, *Dragon Warrior*, was released in 1986. Nintendo, the company that makes it, now only releases new versions on holidays and weekends. Otherwise too many people take time off from work and school to play.

Online video gaming connects players around the world. *PlayerUnknown's Battlegrounds* regularly tops 1 million gamers at any one time, according to the SteamCharts website. Its peak was just over 3 million players in December 2017. That record probably won't last long.

app—a program that is downloaded to computers and mobile devices; app is short for application

CHAPTER 3

COOL CHARACTER FACTOIDS

One of the best parts of playing video games is that you can become your favorite character. But have you ever wondered how these characters came to be?

Sega designers wanted a fierce but loveable character for a new game. It came down to an armored armadillo or a spiky hedgehog. *Sonic the Hedgehog* won that battle. He has been winning ever since. Naoto Ohshima designed *Sonic the Hedgehog.* How did he come up with the design? He says he put Felix the Cat's head on Mickey Mouse's body.

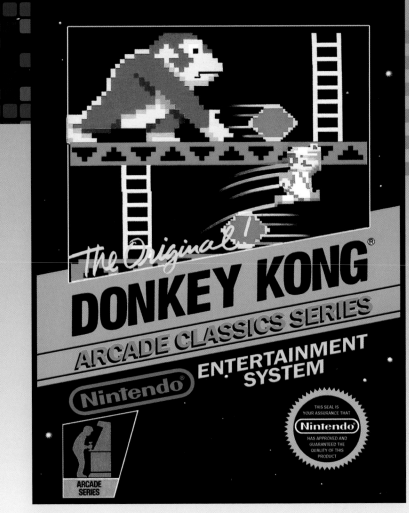

Designers wanted to create a new game featuring Popeye the Sailor. His opponent would be his muscle-bound rival Bluto. But Nintendo could not get permission to use these classic cartoon characters. Who did they create instead? They came up with *Donkey Kong*. The big ape faced off against a plumber with a floppy red hat and big mustache. You may have heard of him and his brother, Luigi. Today, Mario is the most recognizable character in video game history.

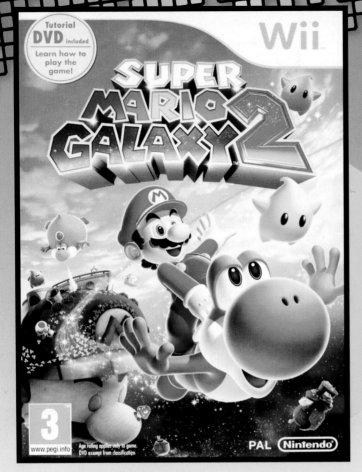

Bonus trivia: When Mario's character was being developed, his original name was "Jumpman." And he wasn't a plumber. He was a carpenter.

Super Mario Galaxy includes a surprise **unlockable character**. Mario is the hero, as usual. He must rescue his taller, greener brother, Luigi. But if players accomplish certain goals they unlock Luigi. They can then play as a super-powered version of him. All it takes is collecting 120 stars and defeating Bowser in combat.

unlockable character—a hidden character a player must win the right to play

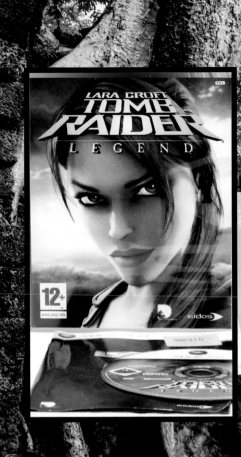

Lara Croft is one of the most popular video game heroes in history. At least 10 versions of the game have been made. In 2001 *Lara Croft: Tomb Raider* became the top-selling movie based on a video game character. In 2018 a new version of the film came out.

The Temple of Ta Prohm, made famous by *Tomb Raider*

Sackboy is the good guy of *LittleBigPlanet*. This quirky game lets players create and share new game levels. Sackboy zips around collecting bubbles and dressing up in the things he finds. He also proves there's more to being a hero than knocking out opponents. At the end, he faces his "boss fight"—a final big battle. His foe is The Collector. However, The Collector just turns out to be a lonely guy. Sackboy wins the game by offering friendship.

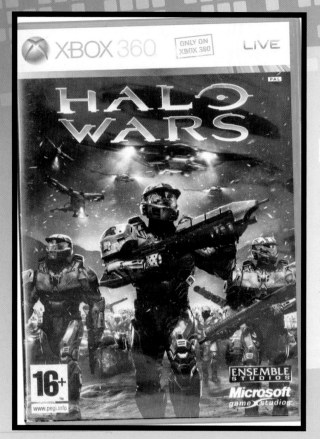

Master Chief is the super-soldier in the *Halo* series. Game maker sources describe his character as standing about 7 feet (2.13 meters) tall. In his powered armor, he weighs 1,000 pounds (450 kilograms).

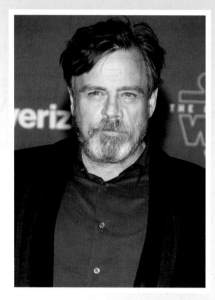

Actor Mark Hamill is most famous for playing Luke Skywalker in the *Star Wars* movies. But for the game *Batman: Arkham City*, he went to the dark side. He voiced Batman's arch enemy, the Joker. Hamill perfected Joker's well-known crazy laugh.

Tony Hawk's *Pro Skater* collection features a few of the weirdest guest characters in gaming. Players can skate as Shrek, Benjamin Franklin, and Spider-man. They can also choose to be a giant hand and other weird objects.

CHAPTER 4

FROM VIRTUAL TO REALITY

Today, video games are much more than fun and games. They have become part of popular culture and everyday life.

Video games are fun for the whole family. Almost six out of 10 parents play video games with their kids, according to the Entertainment Software Association. About 60 percent of players play with friends.

Do you think video games are just for kids? Think again! Today, the average gamer is about 30 years old. Almost 30 percent of adults older than 50 play video games.

Worldwide, there are more than 2 billion gamers. They have turned video games into a huge industry that earns almost $100 billion a year. That total is more than the music and movie industries combined.

The military uses video game technology to train its soldiers and sailors. Even medics learn certain skills using **simulations**. Battle simulations let them train to handle dangerous situations. In a game, they do not have to risk their lives or blow up anything real.

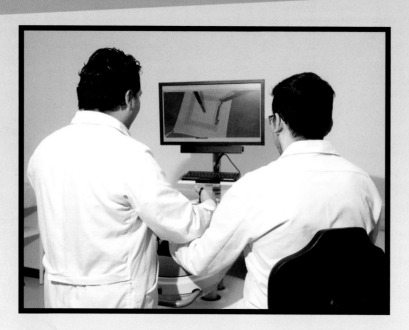

Video games can help surgeons improve their game at work. Laparoscopic surgery puts a camera and surgical tools inside a patient through a small cut. A 2003 study compared laparoscopic surgeons who regularly played video games to those who didn't. The gamers operated faster. They also made fewer mistakes than the other group.

More employers are using video game technology to train workers. Simulators let pilots practice flying aircraft. Software also teaches people to **navigate** huge ships, put out fires, and operate giant construction cranes. The programs can simulate all kinds of weather. These simulators let people practice their duties without any real-life risk.

simulation—a computer model of something in real life

navigate—to steer a course

Gamescom is the biggest gaming convention in the world. In 2017 it drew more than 350,000 video game fans from 106 countries. More than 900 companies showed off their coolest games.

Video Games Live™ organizes international concerts. They perform music from popular video games. The orchestra plays songs from *Warcraft*, *Diablo*, *Myst*, and dozens of other fan favorites. As audience members listen, they see images from the games on large screens. This music series has been performed in cities around the world. Thanks to video streaming, 752,109 people saw the show performed in China in 2015. It set a Guinness World Record for this type of concert.

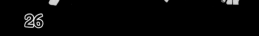

Some video games may help you relax and even get to sleep. Have you ever played *Tetris*? Studies show it can reduce stress and help people sleep.

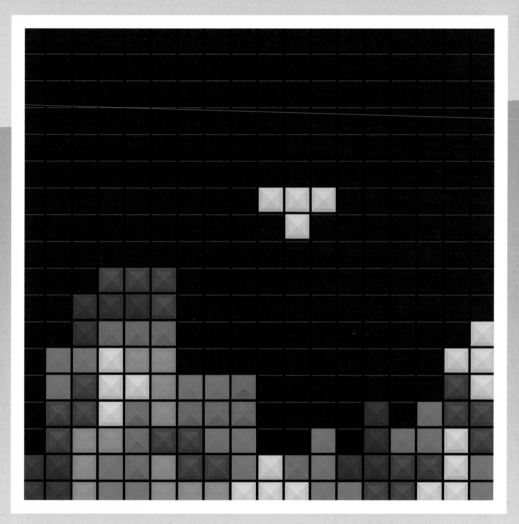

CHAPTER 5

THE NEXT FRONTIER

Video games and gaming grow and change very quickly. New technology and fresh ideas appear constantly.

"**Augmented reality** mobile experiences" take players outside. Games such as *Pokémon GO* and *Harry Potter: Wizards Unite*, let gaming technology interact with the real world.

augmented reality—an enhanced image or environment as viewed on a screen or other display

Game-design technology helped create the Dallas Cowboys Stadium. Computer software let architects view the football field from every angle before it was built. This technology helps builders see possibilities and problems before they start building.

Some game developers are inviting players to help add to their games. These games include software tools so players can develop their own levels and twists. Players can then share their work online.

Video gaming has become a popular spectator sport. The International 7 gaming tournament in 2017 drew more than 20 million viewers. The International Olympic Committee is even considering adding eSports to the Olympic Games.

From *Bertie the Brain* to *Final Fantasy* and beyond, video gaming continues to change. It has grown from simple entertainment to a creative wonderland. The technology knows no limits. It is a source of real-world inspiration as well as fantastic fun.

Glossary

app (APP)—a useful program that is downloaded to computers and mobile devices; app is short for application

arcade (ar-KADE)—a business with video games that you pay to use

architect (AR-ki-tekt)—a person who designs buildings and advises in their construction

augmented reality (AWG-men-tuhd ree-AL-uh-tee)—an enhanced image or environment as viewed on a screen or other display

found (FOUND)—to set up or start something

graphic (GRA-fik)—a visual image such as an illustration, photograph, or work of art

navigate (NAV-uh-gate)—to steer a course

reboot (ree-BOOT)—to start something again

simulation (sim-yuh-LAY-shuhn)—a computer model of something in real life

sound card (SOUND CARD)—computer hardware that allows software programs to produce sounds

unlockable character (un-LOCK-uh-buhl KAYR-ik-tuhr)—a hidden character a player must win the right to play

Read More

Bard, Jonathan. *Video Game Developer.* Behind the Scenes with Coders. New York: PowerKids Press, 2018.

Cunningham, Kevin. *Video Game Designer.* Cool STEAM Careers Ann Arbor, Mich.: Cherry Lake Publishing, 2016.

Kaplan, Arie. *The Awesome Inner Workings of Video Games.* Games and Gamers. Minneapolis: Lerner Publications Company, 2014.

Internet Sites

Use FactHound to find Internet sites related to this book.

Visit *www.facthound.com*

Just type in 9781543525274 and go.

Check out projects, games and lots more at
www.capstonekids.com

Index

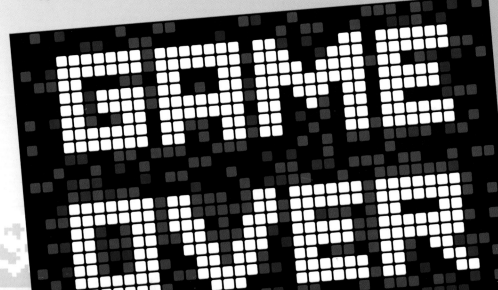